# WHAT ARE KEYSTONE SPECIES?

# BEES
## A WORLDWIDE KEYSTONE SPECIES

KATHLEEN A. KLATTE

PowerKiDS press

Published in 2025 by The Rosen Publishing Group, Inc.
2544 Clinton Street, Buffalo, NY 14224

Copyright © 2025 by The Rosen Publishing Group, Inc.

All rights reserved.

No part of this book may be reproduced in any form without permission in writing from the publisher, except by a reviewer.

First Edition

Editor: Theresa Emminizer
Book Design: Tanya Dellaccio Keeney

Photo Credits: Cover TiagoLuiz/Shutterstock.com; p. 5 Volodymyr Maksymchuk/Shutterstock.com; p. 7 Cornel Constantin/Shutterstock.com; p. 9 media-ja/Shutterstock.com; p. 11 Sakurra/Shutterstock.com; p. 13 weter78/Shutterstock.com; p. 15 OlegD/Shutterstock.com; p. 17 Daniel Prudek/Shutterstock.com; p. 19 Vlad Siaber/Shutterstock.com; p. 21 Andy119/Shutterstock.com.

Cataloging-in-Publication Data
Names: Klatte, Kathleen A.
Title: Bees: a worldwide keystone species / Kathleen A. Klatte.
Description: Buffalo, NY : PowerKids Press, 2025. | Series: What are keystone species? | Includes glossary and index.
Identifiers: ISBN 9781499446562 (pbk.) | ISBN 9781499446579 (library bound) | ISBN 9781499446586 (ebook)
Subjects: LCSH: Bees–Juvenile literature. | Bees–Ecology–Juvenile literature. | Bees–Effect of human beings on–Juvenile literature. | Keystone species–Juvenile literature.
Classification: LCC QL565.2 K525 2025 | DDC 595.79'9–dc23

Manufactured in the United States of America

Some of the images in this book illustrate individuals who are models. The depictions do not imply actual situations or events.

CPSIA Compliance Information: Batch #CSPK25. For further information contact Rosen Publishing at 1-800-237-9932.

# CONTENTS

BUSY BEES .................................................. 4
A WORLD OF BUGS ........................................ 6
SO MANY BEES! ............................................ 8
LIFE IN A HIVE ............................................. 10
JUST BUZZING AROUND ................................ 12
WHERE DO THEY LIVE? ................................. 14
WHAT'S BAD FOR BEES? ............................... 16
NOT JUST HONEY ........................................ 18
BEES ARE OUR FRIENDS ............................... 20
GLOSSARY ................................................. 22
FOR MORE INFORMATION ............................. 23
INDEX ...................................................... 24

# BUSY BEES

Did you know that bees are some of the most important animals on Earth? They pollinate most of the plants in the world. Without bees, many plants couldn't **reproduce**. The plants would die. The animals that eat the plants would go hungry.

People would have to find other ways to make all the things that come from plants. These include food, wood, paper, and fibers to make cloth. Many of the things you use every day wouldn't be here without bees.

## IN FACT!
BEES TAKE POLLEN FROM ONE FLOWER AND MOVE IT TO ANOTHER FLOWER OF THE SAME KIND. THIS IS HOW THE FLOWER MAKES SEEDS. THE SEEDS GROW INTO NEW FLOWERS.

BEES ARE A KEYSTONE SPECIES. THAT MEANS THEY'RE A KIND OF ANIMAL THAT'S VERY IMPORTANT TO THE HABITAT, OR NATURAL HOME, IN WHICH THEY LIVE.

# A WORLD OF BUGS

Bees are insects. Insects are the largest group of animals on Earth. Scientists have identified, or named, about 1 million different kinds of insects. They're found all over the world. They live in hot places, cold places, wet places, and dry places.

Insects have six legs and a set of antennae. Their bodies are made up of three main parts. Instead of having a skeleton inside their body, like people, insects have a hard covering outside their body. This is called an exoskeleton.

### IN FACT!
INSECTS BELONG TO AN EVEN BIGGER GROUP OF ANIMALS CALLED ARTHROPODS. THIS GROUP INCLUDES SPIDERS, LOBSTERS, AND CRABS.

BEES HAVE TWO SETS OF EYES. THE BIG EYES YOU CAN SEE EASILY ARE CALLED **COMPOUND** EYES. THEY ALSO HAVE A SET OF SIMPLE EYES ON THE TOP OF THEIR HEAD.

# SO MANY BEES!

There are more than 20,000 different species, or kinds, of bees. The most familiar bees are honeybees and bumblebees. They're black and yellow or black and orange. However, there are also blue bees. Some bees in South America don't have stingers. Instead, they keep themselves safe by biting.

The largest bee species is called Wallace's giant bee. (Don't worry—it's not really giant!) It has a wingspan, or wing length, of 2.5 inches (6.4 cm). Wallace's giant bees live in Indonesia.

**IN FACT!**

MANY BEES EAT POLLEN OR DRINK NECTAR FROM FLOWERS. HOWEVER, SOME KINDS EAT FRUIT. OTHER KINDS EAT DEAD ANIMALS.

CARPENTER BEES LIKE TO **BURROW** INTO WOOD TO MAKE THEIR NESTS.

# LIFE IN A HIVE

About 2,000 species of bees are social. That means they live in groups called colonies. The colony builds a nest to live in and store food.

There are three kinds of bees in a colony—a queen, workers, and drones. There is only one queen bee in a nest. She's the only one who can have babies. The workers are female bees who help take care of the nest and the baby bees. Drones are male bees. There are fewer drones than worker bees.

BEES GO THROUGH FOUR BIG CHANGES AS THEY GROW UP. THEY START OUT AS AN EGG. THE NEXT STAGE IS A LARVA—SORT OF LIKE A TINY WORM. THE LARVA TURNS INTO A PUPA. THE PUPA GROWS INTO AN ADULT BEE.

## HONEYBEE LIFE CYCLE

1. EGG
2. LARVAE
3. PUPA
4. ADULT BEE

# JUST BUZZING AROUND

Bees spend most of their time collecting food. Honeybees drink nectar from flowers. Then they return to their nest and turn the nectar into honey. They store the honey and feed it to their young. Honeybees also make beeswax. They use it to build the honeycombs in their nest where they store honey and raise their young.

Other kinds of bees eat pollen. They fly from flower to flower collecting pollen. They bring the pollen back to the nest to feed to their young.

**IN FACT!**
THE BUZZING NOISE BEES MAKE IS THE SOUND OF THEIR WINGS BEATING VERY QUICKLY. THIS BUZZ HELPS SOME KINDS OF FLOWERS RELEASE THEIR POLLEN.

# WHERE DO THEY LIVE

Bees live on every **continent** besides Antarctica. Antarctica is the continent located at the South Pole. There are very few plants that can survive the harsh **climate**. It's much too cold for bees to survive.

Bees can survive in places that have winter by preparing all through the rest of the year. They make lots of honey and store it in their nest. When it gets colder, the queen bee stops laying eggs. The worker bees bunch together to keep the nest warm.

BEES MUST MAKE MANY POUNDS OF HONEY TO FEED THE COLONY THROUGH THE WINTER.

# WHAT'S BAD FOR BEES?

Scientists believe that **populations** of about half the species of bees in North America are dropping. They think some kinds might even become **extinct**.

There are lots of reasons for this. One is pesticides. These are **chemicals** people spray to kill bugs and animals that harm crops or make people sick. The problem is pesticides don't just kill the animals that bother people—they can also kill good insects like bees. Pesticides can also make birds sick.

## IN FACT!

BEES DO BEST WHEN THEY HAVE LOTS OF DIFFERENT FLOWERS TO GET NECTAR AND POLLEN FROM. PEOPLE LIKE TO PLANT WHOLE FIELDS OF JUST ONE SPECIES. THIS ISN'T A GOOD DIET FOR BEES.

A GOLF COURSE IS A VERY UNHEALTHY PLACE FOR WILDLIFE. ALL THAT GRASS IS THE SAME SPECIES. IT TAKES LOTS OF PESTICIDES AND WEED KILLER TO KEEP IT THAT WAY.

# NOT JUST HONEY

    People have practiced beekeeping for thousands of years. They raise bees in a place called an apiary. Apiaries are kept safe and warm. People collect the extra honey and wax that the bees make.

    Farmers also place bees in fields to pollinate trees and plants. This helps bring in a successful crop. Honeybees are the most important pollinator of crops for sale in the United States. Over 100 different crops need them to grow. Without bees, there would be fewer fresh fruits and vegetables.

IF A CROP FAILS, THERE WON'T BE AS MUCH OF THAT KIND OF FOOD. WHAT'S AVAILABLE WILL BE PRICEY.

## IN FACT!

WITHOUT BEES TO POLLINATE THEIR PLANTS, A FARMER'S CROPS MIGHT FAIL. THE FARMER WOULDN'T BE ABLE TO PAY THEIR BILLS. THEY MIGHT NOT BE ABLE TO PAY FOR SEEDS TO PLANT THE NEXT YEAR.

# BEES ARE OUR FRIENDS

Bees pollinate one out of every three bites of food we eat. Without them, many people would go hungry. Without bees, farmers would be out of work and food would cost more money.

People can help bees by being very careful about the kinds of chemicals they use in their yards. Even better, they can replace lawns with native wildflower gardens. Wildflowers are colorful and smell good. They attract birds, bees, and butterflies.

WILDFLOWERS DON'T NEED A LOT OF **FERTILIZER** OR PESTICIDES TO GROW. THIS IS HEALTHIER FOR PEOPLE TOO.

# GLOSSARY

**burrow:** To dig a hole in the ground for shelter.
**chemical:** Matter that can be mixed with other matter to cause changes.
**climate:** The usual weather conditions in a particular place or region.
**compound:** Something that is formed by combining two or more parts.
**continent:** One of Earth's seven great landmasses.
**extinct:** No longer existing.
**fertilizer:** Something added to the soil to help plants grow.
**population:** The number of animals in a species that live in a place.
**reproduce:** To produce babies, young animals, new plants, etc.

# FOR MORE INFORMATION

## BOOKS

Jacobson, Bray. *Bees*. New York, NY: Gareth Stevens Publishing, 2022.

Press, J.P. *Bees*. Minneapolis, MN: Bearport Publishing Company, 2023.

## WEBSITES

### The Bee Conservancy
*thebeeconservancy.org/bee-activities-for-kids*
Check out the Bee Conservancy's page of free fun kids' activities.

### National Geographic Kids
*www.natgeokids.com/au/discover/animals/insects/honey-bees/*
Learn 10 facts about honey bees!

**Publisher's note to educators and parents:** Our editors have carefully reviewed these websites to ensure that they are suitable for students. Many websites change frequently, however, and we cannot guarantee that a site's future contents will continue to meet our high standards of quality and educational value. Be advised that students should be closely supervised whenever they access the internet.

# INDEX

**A**
Antarctica, 14

antennae, 6

apiary, 18

arthropod, 6

**C**
colony, 10, 15

**D**
drones, 10

**E**
exoskeleton, 6

**I**
Indonesia, 8

insect, 6

**P**
pesticides, 16, 17, 21

pollinate, 4, 18, 20

pupa, 11

**W**
Wallace's giant bee, 8

workers, 10, 14